MW00978712

Workhealing

*W*orkhealing

The Healing Process
for You and Your Job

CHARLES MALLORY

DeVorss *Publications*

ISBN:0-87516-664-4
Library of Congress Catalog Card Number: 93-73675

First Edition, 1993

DeVorss & Company, Publisher
P.O. Box 550
Marina del Rey, CA 90294

Printed in the United States of America

*W*orkhealing
Table of Contents

> *The Law of Acceptance:* I accept my feeling about
> my work without judging the people, tasks,
> or environment.
> *The Law of Divine Order:* All things will have their right
> outcome, and I will be divinely guided to be involved or
> to let go during the process.
> *The Law of Gratitude:* Regardless of my situation, I say,
> "All I see is opportunity."

> —Use affirmations and simple positive techniques to
> move yourself forward in the process.

**Dedicated to
John-Mark and Max**

Workhealing

Part One

ACHIEVING WORK WHOLENESS

1

New Vistas

*T*here are times when work hurts. Personalities clash, multiple priorities vie for time, and bosses seem to crack whips. We feel stressed, angry, sullen, self-hating, sorrowful...

But work is a necessary evil, we tell ourselves. Even in a job one likes, there are those mundane or unpleasant duties that must be faced.

We may respond to negative job experiences in the typical ways, disliking everyday life or letting the work problem permeate home life. Or we begin a job-hunt, looking for a magic escape. Whether the job problems are caused by inward or outward circumstances, they sometimes erupt again on the next job. And off we go again.

Then, when there are so-called "tough" economic times, fewer jobs seem available and distressed workers feel stuck.

We've seen evidence of job problems in our bodies and minds. People go crazy and commit violent acts. More commonly, the stress and job burnout causes health challenges.

Too many of us have worked ourselves into this situation. But it doesn't have to be.

No matter where you work, what your job duties are, or what your boss and co-workers are like, you have a solution. There is a way to push past the negativity and stress of work problems. You can find peace. You can be centered. You can love your life again.

The key is to NOT make major changes, such as a job-hunt, financial commitment, new education or training, or other alteration in your life, until you have *workhealed* yourself.

Workhealing is to bind the wounds inflicted at work, using self-recovery to pull yourself out of the mire and move ahead—swiftly, surely and successfully—to a new state of being.

Does this sound comforting to you? It should, because it is a comforting process. Our concern is not to make ourselves more productive or to gain new career directions. It is only to heal our work situation. Work is a marvelous channel for us to use our energy and knowledge for building a better world. Yet too often, detrimental factors keep us from being as productive and happy as we would like. Maybe others who don't like to work try to make us feel terrible because of their own problems. Perhaps one who has a need for power hurts others to achieve that power. Yet another person might get misaligned enjoyment from seeing others unhappy.

Work has been with humankind since the dawn of earth's history. We are far from the days of our work consisting of hunting and killing wild animals for food. We are also far from future work—when minds will do virtually everything, with perhaps only our fingers or voices needed to activate computers and robots.

Work has been with us since the beginning of time, and will stay with us until our only "work" is to be pure forms of spiritual beings, existing in a perfect universe.

Work is here to stay. That's why counting on having time off as a respite is only a temporary measure. We will work for much of our lives and must make the most of it. This is a good aspect of life, though, because fulfilling work is a joy to the soul and a thrill to the mind and body. Even overcoming a work challenge is an accomplishment to be proud of. If we begin the process with workhealing, we can reach that new vista of enjoying life—every aspect of life, including work!

What about the "down" times, though? Aren't they inevitable?

No. There is no rule that says a job can't be enjoyable every minute of the day. Maybe we've considered work a necessary evil to get money, which helps us function in our world. The term "necessary evil" is completely wrong. It's not only not evil, it's a glorious opportunity.

A popular TV commercial touted a radio station that played easy-listening music. The commercial said, "Play our radio station all day at work—it'll make the workday go faster." Is that your mentality? Do you simply want the workday to go by as fast as possible? Do you count the hours, even the minutes? Do you anticipate the weekend, knowing you'll be away from work, and then the weekend passes too fast?

If so, change your mind and change your life. Work

doesn't have to be a great dark void in your life, a time to be passed through on the way to more enjoyable times. You can elevate it to a higher plateau. It begins within.

In this manual on workhealing, you will forgive, *even bless,* a difficult boss or uncooperative co-workers. Instead of thinking about the lack at your job, you will think, *All I see is opportunity.* Rather than seeing roadblocks and disagreements at work, you will see a clear, illumined path just for you. You will smooth over the rough edges caused by work and glide to a new, better place in your heart—a place that can withstand the challenges of your current job and give you the guidance, timing and opportunity to make a new path for the future.

BRINGING BELIEF TO BUSINESS

You might wonder, "How could I have gotten this negative about work?"

It can happen to anyone, including those of us striving to reach the highest and best way of life. We might excel in other areas of life while still viewing work in somewhat negative fashion. We might try to separate our work and home personalities. They can't truly be separated, though. Our work persona isn't different skin that we shed at the workplace after we punch the time clock or walk out the door. Your job is more part of you than you might realize.

That person is you at the cash register; trading securities; piloting the plane; teaching the pupils; selling the products; tending the sick. Just as our work seems to hurt us because we carry a difficult work situation home, we also imbue our work with the distinct personality we possess. Yes, it's true, no matter what you do!

A job has an effect on us because we have an effect on it. That's why when things go wrong, we feel wronged. You are not your job, but work truly is a constant interchange between our tasks and our selves.

Don't berate yourself if your leanings toward a positive way of life haven't been as effective in the work arena. For quite some time, humankind has made little connection between work and spiritual pursuits.

CONSIDER THESE THINGS:

• **How many times have you heard a minister discuss the connection between the spiritual self and work?**

• **How many Bible verses specifically advise us on handling work situations in God's way?**

• **Most people consider only the work of ministers, missionaries, faith healers and such others as "working for God."**

Are you working for God? Of course you are, if you are in any legitimate job situation ("legitimate" means a legal job not designed to hurt others). If you sell lawn sprinklers, what you do helps keep grass green and beautiful. That's helping the wonderful creation of the universe. Think of what you do. You can likely see how it improves a world created by God (God, Allah, Buddha, Higher One, Nature, or whatever you call your Creator). Many of us have never been told that our jobs help perpetuate the improvement of our world. But they do. And throughout our lives we have dramatic opportunities to improve our world.

There are "gray areas" concerning jobs. If you work in a nuclear power plant, are you advancing God's world or hurting it? Look in your heart. If you believe you are creating a safe energy source, you are advancing God's world. If you do not believe you are doing right, you need to switch jobs to help you retain the belief that you are advancing God's world. Illegal employment, such as selling illegal drugs, obviously is not the right track to advancing God's world. Even if you believe something that is illegal should be legal, remember that divine order sets the order for all—our laws are as they are for a reason. If something is wrong, it will be changed in time.

"Divine order" is a marvelous concept that few people have yet understood. More and more people are grasping it, though. Divine order means things occur *as* they should *when* they should. You've seen someone shake their head and sorrowfully say, "It wasn't meant to be." Or tell about a joyous, serendipitous situation and say, "It was meant to be!" Divine order is that mysterious "clock" that sets everything in motion at the exact right time—without fail. The more we become attuned to our own great powers within, the more in tune we are with divine order.

What about factory jobs? If you work on an assembly line, making small plastic parts for cars, are you really advancing this world? Yes! You are helping create a reliable and enjoyable mode of transportation. What if you sell septic tanks? Yes! You're helping immeasurably—what would some people do without them? What if you type index cards for an obscure reference library? Yes! You are helping others gain knowledge.

Yes, we *are* pushing creation forth, advancing the world created by God, to make lives for all beings productive and fun. We are part of the creation process. YOU are part of this ever-advancing, evergreen process.

Certainly there are days when our jobs prove difficult and seem to be helping everything but the process of creation. There are days when we feel lax. But we are producing. This makes each person in a legitimate job a worker for God. Whether you are a construction worker, secretary or president of a large corporation, you are assisting in the creation of this universe, with your job as holy as anyone's!

Knowing this might magnify the negative feelings you've gained about work. After all, you might be "hating" the very thing that helps advance God's world! But don't magnify these thoughts; you are human, and such progressions are natural. Just as you create through your work, you also have the divine ability to workheal yourself out of a negative work situation.

BUT WHAT ABOUT...?

What about the feeling that others have an easier job? Or thinking about celebrities who make millions because of their personalities and fame? Or the feeling that one's talent lies unused and the right job is out there, elsewhere? Those feelings arise in many people. What about the injustice of being mistreated by others at work?

I have been there. I have been in jobs I hated, working with disagreeable people. I have had bosses who pressured relentlessly and managed without reward. I've endured stress that seemed insurmountable, near-drowned in fears about not succeeding, and felt lack at paycheck time. I've worked in a variety of jobs in: a fast-food restaurant, factory, bookstore, publishing company, and public-relations agency. Now I am self-employed, the fulfillment of my work goals.

Interestingly, I've heard many people say they want to be self-employed and it's obvious that they believe they'll be "in control" of their work situation and other people once they achieve this. However, self-employment is simply another job driven by our own creativity and motivation. You must always deal with other people and challenging situations.

Quite simply, I would not write this book, and would not have the privilege of writing this book, unless I had worked in a variety of professions and experienced negative situations at work.

I have also workhealed myself. My eventual solution was to have my own business. But before that, before assessing my options, networking with others, planning on a business, had to come one process: the process of workhealing. For others, before the job search, developing the resume, going on the interview, has to come the workhealing.

The pressures of the past can arise again if you haven't healed previous wounds from work. Even if you have gone through the healing process, you might land in a situation of great challenge. Even so, the workhealing techniques will guide you to thrive under even the most difficult work circumstances.

Whether your low-quality experiences have been caused by yourself or others, you will be able to workheal yourself calmly and easily. The reality of work might not seem to change at first, but when you are at work, you'll be encased in a new, confident shell that will protect you. The new glow, the new confidence, will benefit you.

Your continued efforts at workhealing will then actually change the reality at work, if that is meant to be. As has been said, "Thoughts are things, and thoughts have wings." Powerful affirmations, meaningful prayer, positive readings and other techniques, blended with your deep desire to convert bad to good, can really transcend one's personal mindset to go forth and shape the world.

ACTION NOW

In all likelihood, you're reading this because you're in a debilitating work situation and want relief. Let's get started right now.

Before we discuss the steps in workhealing in Chapter 2, use the affirmations below to begin the healing process. Affirmations are short, positive statements to read and then to let penetrate into your mind. Re-read these as often as you like. Copy them for reading at work, or audiotape them for listening.

Do not be concerned whether the affirmations apply to your specific situation. Simply let them grow and be part of you. If you read them silently, listen to the voice within. Feel the words imbue you with refreshing relief and a new-growing personal strength.

LET'S AFFIRM

**DIFFICULTIES ARE LEAVING ME NOW.
I FEEL RENEWED AND REFRESHED.**

**THOSE WHO APPEAR TO DISAGREE WITH
ME ARE WORKING THROUGH APPEAR-
ANCES ONLY. AGREEMENT AND CALM
WILL RISE BEFORE ME.**

**I SEE THE GOOD IN ALL THINGS. I LOOK
PAST WHAT I'VE SEEN BEFORE—THE SUR-
FACE, THE ARTIFICIAL COVERING—AND
SEE THE TRUE GOOD THAT IS AT THE
CORE OF ALL THINGS.**

**I FEEL RENEWAL NOW, SWEET RENEWAL,
FLOODING ME AND PERMEATING EVERY
FIBER OF MY BEING. CALM, EASY WAVES
OF REST WASH OVER ME.**

2

The Three Laws

*C*ongratulations! You've begun the workhealing process by inviting peace, love and divine order into your life. Just asking for that change brings about the beginning of your success.

To continue on your workhealing, it is necessary to understand the "Three Laws" that govern workhealing. They are in sequential order. They are stepping-stones to a complete healing of your work situation, a full sense of peace for yourself.

The Law of Acceptance: I accept my feelings about my work without judging the people, tasks or environment.

The Law of Divine Order: All things will have the right outcome, and I will be divinely guided to be involved or to let go during the process.

The Law of Gratitude: Regardless of my situation, I say, "All I see is opportunity." Opportunity is all around me and within.

These Three Laws reflect all the truth that exists in any

work situation. Other negative elements are only appearances, not direction of a Higher Power for advancing our world. Your worries and fears about the outcome are useless, because divine order will direct all anyway. So get into the flow and let go of your troubles.

What do these Three Laws really mean? Let's take a closer look.

THE LAW OF ACCEPTANCE

I accept my feelings about my work without judging the people, tasks or environment.

Much denial occurs at work. On the first day of a much-desired new job, we believe that is this the perfect job and that we'll be happy. That's great, because in some cases it comes true! But in other situations, even when we've started out with optimism, we have difficult times and turn to self-blame:

"I should have brought up this problem sooner."

"Maybe he'll quit or get fired—then everything will be okay."

"Perhaps the company will have a better financial picture next year and I'll get a bonus."

"I ought to have blown the whistle on that situation."

We turn to many "I should haves," "I oughts" and other statements. We believe that next week, next month or even next year, some magical or different occurrence will erase the obstacle and our work will be better. We plan on the departures of some people or the arrival of new, better co-workers.

12

Yes, in some instances these things happen. In some cases, the problem stems from within and we do not see it. At times, we don't even look within, think affirmatively about the situation, but rather wait for some genie to appear and remove the obstacle for us. Some of us realize we're doing this. Some of us even know that we have the power and ability we need to change our lives! Yet we don't take this important step.

We often turn to blame, too. It's that person's fault, it's my new cubicle, it's the difficult period the company is going through, etc. Remember, we have the ability to make our own pathway in life—so why do we direct negative energy toward others in the form of blame or criticism? Why do we direct negative energy toward ourselves in the form of blame and self-criticism?

We end up burdening ourselves with what we now label as a "bad job," an albatross to be worn around the neck until 5 P.M.!

Get past the blaming of others and blaming yourself. Get past *all* the blame. Do not crowd yourself with "I should have," "I ought to have," and "This will somehow change." Likewise, do not say, "It's my boss who is the problem" or "If I had different co-workers, I'd be happier."

Simply *accept!* Accept your feelings about your work. Do you *feel* negative about it? That's okay—you only *feel* negative. That does not mean your work situation *is* negative. Your feelings are there, they are something you are handling, and you can accept that you have these feelings. The negativity only has a face value, not real value.

Do not judge others. Lay aside all blame, though it might be tempting to hold onto it. Wipe away the past.

You have accepted your feelings. Your goal is to become centered about your work and to seek divine direction. Let all else go. By letting go, you empower yourself.

THE LAW OF DIVINE ORDER

All things will have the right outcome, and I will be divinely guided to be involved or to let go during the process.

In talking with others about negative work situations, you'll hear such statements as:

"It's not fair!"

"His assistant is certainly his pet!"

"This is really a Good Ol' Boy network."

"I can't believe the way she handled things!"

When work doesn't feel great for us, injustice seems to abound. Sometimes that injustice seems to really exist in a situation—but what we really don't perceive or understand is the true temporary nature of that injustice as divine order is unfolding. Other times we have magnified what is a small fracture in the normally smooth-working patterns of justice, or we have dreamed up a situation that is not really unfair at all.

A seeming lack of justice might have happened to you. Some ways this might occur:

— A supervisor, trying to save on the budget, gives you an unfairly low-graded performance review.

—You've done a good job and someone else

takes (and gets) the credit.

—You're part of a team project and accused of not carrying your weight on the project, though you have.

—An aggressive person in the office uses you to get ahead.

There are many more ways that injustice can seem to occur. Typical ways we handle it are to be hurt, mad or to feel jealous. One who is more sensitive can be especially harmed by this type of situation.

You've probably noticed that I continue to use the phrase "seeming injustice" in this section. It appears as injustice to us, but in the Greater World there is no injustice—all imperfections are merely blips on the screen of life, as everything progresses through divine order.

Think about it. Haven't you had many situations that "worked out for the best"? You might have had situations that you didn't think worked out for the best or which aren't resolved yet! But divine order is still moving forward, working through the process.

I recall in one job having a tremendously difficult project that seemed to have no end. Because I am a writer, perhaps a need for project completion is overly important for me; I know I am extra-sensitive to such a situation. I remember trying to believe that this was a trial or exercise I had to go through that would somehow benefit me. But as the negative experience wore on, with poor results, I gave hard thought to the purpose of the experience. I could see no benefit whatsoever in going through it. It had no bearing on what I wanted to do in the future.

A few years later, I had the opportunity to go through the same process in my own business. Had I not had the earlier experience, I would have accepted the assignment. As it was, I knew what was ahead of me and chose not to accept it. It involved working closely with a very dominant person, working long hours and traveling extensively. It also involved working with someone who wanted me to help but did not want my professional opinion and expertise on the subject. This would have been my sole project for a period of three or four months and I would have possibly lost other clients because I wouldn't have been able to help them during that time period.

I know beyond the shadow of a doubt that if I hadn't had the on-the-job experience (and known how negatively I would respond to such a work situation), I would have taken it, because the project would have paid $20,000+. So my experience finally paid off. All of your experiences have a purpose, and if the purpose has not yet been shown to you, have patience.

So seeming injustice really does move past itself and get resolved. That is because you are your true boss. We give entirely too much attention to the supervisor-subordinate relationship. We are to follow our boss's instructions (when they're not misguided instructions), but a human supervisor is merely a person of temporary guidance here on earth.

Since we are all helping advance a world created by a Higher Power, you are your true boss in every situation. You have the divine spark within that guides your life. Obviously, we can't shirk our human bosses because of this. Imagine saying to your supervisor, "You're not my boss—*I* am!" But what we can do is place the truth front and center in our lives—that a supervisor is a person of guidance, and that each of us is responsible for his or her own pathway.

Decision-making about a job can plague us. Should I get a new job? Should I stick with this one? Could I get another job? Are times too tight, jobs scarce? Do I have the right training? Can I really adjust to a new job?

There's no need for the grappling and groping with various issues when choosing what to do—for everything has its right outcome.

Will you leave your job? It may not be known yet, but it is known at all times that everything will work out for the best. Will you turn things around on your current job? It may not be known yet, but it is known at all times that everything will work out for the best.

Turn away from the many questions of *where, when* and *how*—how you'll do this or that, or should make this move or that. *It will have its right outcome!* Simply meditate on being peaceful, and let the clock of divine order do its perfect work.

You do not have to force yourself to juggle a multitude of thoughts because a Higher Power is working within you, filling you with insight and peace, making a right outworking come about. You will be divinely guided in what direction to take, and you need not beg for an answer or a sign. The answer is already yours, and it will come in its right time. When it comes, it *will* be the right time, even if you think the right time is sooner!

Divine order is the pattern for all the universe, and you are part of that universe. So all will be well. All works under divine order.

Does it seem as though I am talking in circles? I am, because life is only one big circle, composed entirely of divine order. No matter what direction we think we might be in, we are truly in the direction of divine order.

THE LAW OF GRATITUDE

Regardless of my situation, I think, "All I see is opportunity." Opportunity is all around me and within.

"All I see is opportunity"? When I'm feeling terrible? you might ask.

Yes. Opportunity is everywhere, at all times. It is around, above, beneath and within you. It is not always in your conscious mind; it is not always apparent to you, though it is always there. A clear mind, peace within and centeredness help you achieve sight of these opportunities.

If your boss has said tomorrow is your last day, think,

ALL I SEE IS OPPORTUNITY.

If you haven't gotten a raise for years, think,

ALL I SEE IS OPPORTUNITY.

If your co-workers and supervisor seem to hate you, think,

ALL I SEE IS OPPORTUNITY.

If you dread going to work each morning and don't know how you'll endure the day, think,

ALL I SEE IS OPPORTUNITY.

At this point you might think I'm completely crazy!

18

But remember (and deep within, don't you *know?*) that opportunity is all around you, growing like abundant, beautiful flowers. When your job situation is perfect, opportunity is there. When your job situation is intolerable, opportunity is there.

This has been one of the best single statements I have ever discovered. It is either a prayer or an affirmation, or both at once. In a few words it strongly states, "I believe and I am grateful."

Finding the opportunity is your eventual goal. It is not your goal this very moment. Do not fret over how, where and when you'll find that opportunity. Do not expect to see it at a certain time or place. Do not give it a deadline. It's there all the time and will simply be unfolded before you. Thinking *All I see is opportunity* will bring you closer to whatever you seek. It also has an extra bonus: it helps you become relaxed and centered so that you can erase negativity and enjoy each moment more.

Even if you don't try very hard to seek opportunity but think *All I see is opportunity,* opportunity will find you! For the very act of prayer and saying an affirmation is a powerful tool, and you will bring to yourself what you need and want.

Be grateful for everything. For the little things, for the big things. In any situation, there is at least a seed of truth, understanding and divine direction that will help you. Life is abundant and wonderful, and the more grateful we are, the more wonderful things we see.

Here are linked affirmations for acceptance, divine order, and gratitude:

19

AN INNER AWAKENING IS NOW OCCUR-
RING; I AM MY BEST AND DO MY BEST.

IN THIS GREAT WORLD, THERE IS ONLY
DIVINE ORDER.

MY LIFE IS A GIFT ABUNDANTLY GIVEN.
I WILL LIVE MY APPRECIATION.

GOOD UNFOLDS IN ITS PERFECT WAY
AND AT THE RIGHT TIME.

3

The Clearing Process

After launching your understanding of the Three Laws, it is wise to begin the Clearing Process. The Clearing Process is a technique to help bring about workhealing. In that way, it is your instrument to bring the Three Laws to fulfillment.

Here are the three steps in clearing:

1. **Recognize and accept.**

2. **Eliminate either/or.**

3. **Cancel negative thoughts.**

Now here is the process in an even simpler fashion:

1. **SEE**

2. **OPEN**

3. **CANCEL**

Why these simpler words? Because as you begin to use the process, it becomes complete so quickly that you don't even "think" the three steps. You merely become centered. It's similar to taking a deep breath to relax yourself, or quickly affirming, "divine order." You instantly move from a non-centered experience into true centeredness, and feel an immediate sense of peace.

For workhealing, that quickly instituted flash of centeredness begins with a full understanding of the three things you are doing. Later you will not even acknowledge or try to recognize these three steps; you will quickly transform your negative thought or experience into a feeling of peace.

The outcome of this process is healing. You heal yourself, without a conclusion in mind. You say you are healed and you believe it.

It is after this process that you will begin making decisions and taking actions about your work and your life. You originally asked for workhealing; gained an understanding of the Three Laws; and then will follow the Clearing Process, and you will heal yourself without a conclusion in mind. I do not promise that right after you finish this process the decisions will flash before you. It might happen immediately, or it still might take time.

The first part of the clearing process is to recognize and accept. The situation is there and you are in it. Do not be concerned whether it is "reality" or "appearance." The situation is the situation.

The second part is to eliminate either/or thinking. Do not begin struggling for the answer, thinking this way or that way is right. Make yourself open to the true answer.

The third part is to cancel negative thoughts and experiences. Yes, you can cancel a negative experience because the negativity is your reaction to the experience—it's not reality.

I've used a "canceling" technique that has proven very valuable. Simply think the word *cancel*. Use a simple visualization technique, if you need to, to accompany the thought. You can envision a windshield wiper clearing a window and think, "Cancel." You can visualize walking out of a forest as you suddenly see a beautiful lake in the moonlight—and think, "Cancel."

Use it when negative thoughts hit you or when negative words are coming your way from another! Sometimes you might go for a few seconds or even minutes before you remember to think, "Cancel." Do not worry about it. Simply get in the habit and begin using the process.

If you have a lot of negative thoughts, this process might get very tiring the first day or two. But despite the hassle at first, it becomes easier very quickly. Continue using it, and it becomes second-nature. When a negative thought comes, a sort of thought-eraser automatically activates, gently wiping away the negative thought. Your mind clears freely and without effort, and you go on. It all happens in a split second.

When you try this "cancel" technique, don't be alarmed if you eventually seem to have changed your whole outlook and then have a negative thought return. Or perhaps several will bombard you. Just re-center yourself lovingly, using the process again. It does not mean you have failed, or even slipped, if negative thoughts return. Avoid panic. Avoid belittling yourself. You are more wonderful than you ever imagined. You have more gifts and more grace than you ever imagined. Don't let the process judge you, and don't worry about how "good" you're doing. You're already wonderful. You can master this process.

You can help yourself through very challenging, troubling times with this canceling process. At first the troubling thoughts might be magnified because you're attempting to cancel them. Just remember that they're only "magnified"—appearing larger than before because you're focusing on them.

The canceling process can be used to pass through all three steps at once. Let's say you've heard a rumor that the company is having trouble and that there might be layoffs. You begin to worry. You immediately think, "Cancel," do a visualization if necessary and here's what happens:

1. **SEE—I acknowledge that this rumor occurred.**

2. **OPEN—The right outcome will occur.**

3. **CANCEL—I cancel negative thoughts and am centered.**

BLESSING

Blessing something isn't really a technique, I suppose, just a wonderful, prayerful thing to do. Some people might consider it a "technique" anyway. It's similar to thinking, *All I see is opportunity.*

Blessing is a supplement on your way to workhealing. No matter how much dislike you feel for your job, boss or co-workers, bless your work. Bless that you earn income and skills from it. Follow the idea, *Do not assess, just bless!*

Do not assess whether your income and skills are adequate for what you put into the job—just bless it. Bless your self-development. Don't assess whether you can get better self-development somewhere else, just bless!

This action puts forth more positive feelings in your immediate world and the world at large. It delivers more positive energy in all directions.

It might seem difficult at first to let go of resentment or remembrances of past hurtful actions, but let go. Let go. Let blessings fill you and others. They are blessed, and you are blessed. Forgive, and bless others. Let go of all else.

Bless your work as part of a magnificent creation that you have been chosen to complete. You have been chosen to help complete the creation of the world, no matter how "small" or difficult you think your part in that process is. You have been chosen. Whether you even have a job or not, you have been chosen!

Bless your duties as an opportunity for productivity, rather than idleness; achievement, instead of a void; substance, instead of lack.

HEALING

It is time to heal yourself—remember, without a conclusion in mind. You will easily and freely move through the healing process. Certainly it might not feel "easy" and "free" at times. But it truly is, so know that you can actually be centered during the process.

The following chapters contain advice for healing yourself in a variety of specific situations. Since all work-related challenges are centered in tasks, others, time or substance, you will find something that will help you. Perhaps every page will help you immensely. With each specific topic are affirmations, verses and meditative readings that will bring about deeper understanding. The meditative readings appear on separate pages after each regular chapter text, with areas that pertain to that chapter's issue. When using these readings, you might find it helpful to read them (or a particular one) over and over in a quiet place, then use an affirmation and prayer after.

Some of the verses or affirmations in one chapter might also be pertinent for a different chapter. Use it however you like. Mark in the book or highlight portions as you wish. You cannot read or use this book in an incorrect way, because you're looking at it seeking the truth.

LET'S AFFIRM:

OLD PATTERNS OF NEGATIVITY FALL AWAY FROM ME, AND A NEW, HIGHER WAY EMERGES.

I NOW INFUSE MY SOUL WITH THE BRIGHT MELODY OF PERFECT PEACE.

Part Two

WORKHEALING
YOURSELF

4

Affirmative Thinking

hen you first learn of the ideas I've discussed so far, it's somewhat difficult to
understand the power of affirmations, positive
spoken words, and a strong belief in changing life through
changing your thoughts. Sure, we hope it will happen,
but "practical" thinking takes over and we wonder why
humankind hasn't soared further if it's that simple.

It *is* that simple. Some souls are beginning to learn it
and precious few have fully mastered it. Yet it's true. It's
proven time and time again. We have so much negative
input for many years of our lives. It's virtually impossible
to shut it off, since if you turn on the TV news or have a
negative acquaintance, you often get hit by it instantly.
But we can certainly stem the flow when we want to take
control. And we can fill our mind with beautiful, loving
thoughts...thoughts that will eventually permeate our
being. Our subconscious "you can't do it" is gently erased

and replaced by "you can, you can."

Funny that in sports when a coach or teammates yell, "You can do it!" people believe that the cheer really helps someone succeed. The same people might laugh at the idea of using affirmations or positive-thinking tapes. It's the same process!

I approached the idea of affirmative thinking as reluctantly as anyone. I have now seen it work. I am aware of specific times when my mind thinks, "Yes, you can" where before it said, "You can't."

There have been a number of times when things seemed to move toward a downward slump for me. An example is when my job is harder than usual, friends get busy and social activities decline, and there are hassles—time to pay taxes, the street in front of my house under reconstruction, etc. At such times, I equip myself readily, listening to subliminal tapes in my home office and using affirmation tapes in my car. I heavily focus on turning things right. And they do! Without external circumstances changing, everything brightens up. I don't let the little things get me down, and the resulting positive feeling is generated to others, who respond better to me.

It isn't magic. It's the truth of the universe. This is the way things are supposed to work. We are intended to be a universe of loving, cooperative beings progressing smoothly at all times.

You might well have many times at work when you find that hard to believe. The circumstances might point to an inability to change. You might think, "I can say affirmations, but I really want a new boss." Or, "I don't want to *imagine* my world changing—I really want to *do* something about it!"

With affirmations and other methods to help you think better and more clearly, you will "do something about it." Something, perhaps, more powerful than taking specific outward actions.

There is no doubt that changing your mind can change your life. I received no greater evidence of this than when I worked as an editor at UNITY Magazine. We received letters sent to Silent Unity for possible inclusion in the magazine, and of course, we had lovingly prayed for all of those who had written as we reviewed the letters.

I was astounded at the many positive results in the letters. People wrote about every problem in the book—cancer, neighbors' barking dogs, a child's poor grades, a parent breaking a hip, handling a family death, having mental illness, and anything else you can imagine—and time after time again they overcame it. Many of them simply changed their thinking. It was especially startling to hear of the many, many cancer patients who used affirmations and positive thoughts and went into spontaneous remission. Doctors who had tried every treatment suddenly found their patients healing themselves. Or someone who had "no hope" was suddenly cured.

Once I told a friend about the miracles these letters told of, and he questioned whether I thought they were valid. I said to him, "This month, I've seen more than 1,000 letters. Can they all be lying?"

There were simply too many letters and too much validity and accuracy in the letters for me to disbelieve it. I wish I could parade the scoffers through the Unity offices and let them read these letters by the bundleful. It's truly an awe-inspiring, life-affirming experience.

There's no particular magic to one denomination or religious movement. People of all faiths, or even of no faith, all over the world, are experiencing a Higher Greatness! No matter how we tailor our particular religious beliefs, or fit our concept of a Higher Power within a particular church, we are all experiencing the same great phenomenon. We are merely giving it different names and expressing it in different ways.

No matter how awkward it might feel to you, no matter how much you disbelieve it at this point, use affirmations and uplifting materials that will help you change your mind to change your life.

Remember, you've fed yourself negative statements repeatedly. They become a self-fulfilling prophecy. So take good thoughts and make *those* become a self-fulfilling prophecy!

THE MONDAY-MORNING MEETING

Joe was a perfect example of how this works. He worked in a very stressful job and had a complete turnaround because of affirmations. His work featured a weekly meeting, held before regular work hours on Monday morning. The whole point was to jolt the workers into action at the very beginning of the week. The boss pushed workers to get more done and pointed out shortcomings to various individuals. This was not your uplifting sort of meeting.

Joe's mind was heavy with negative thoughts when he returned to his cubicle after these meetings. He was thinking:

I hate this place!

What a terrible boss!

Why does he single us out for criticism?

All of these thoughts, and the many that followed, are negative self-talk. Joe began to disallow the negative self-talk and filled his thought time with affirmations. He returned from the meetings and silently read affirmations like:

ANXIETY AND WORRY FALL AWAY AS I TURN WITHIN AND ACCEPT PEACE.

MY HEART RELEASES FEELINGS OF TROUBLE AND FILLS WITH THE PEACE OF PATIENCE.

INFINITE GOOD IS ABUNDANTLY MINE. I CLAIM IT NOW.

LET GO AND LET GOD.

Joe became more productive and happier. Outward appearances seemingly had not changed. The meetings were still tough. But they were less tough for Joe, who knew that his mind was his own and that he would walk away and think affirmatively. Soon, the boss had less to criticize about Joe. Perhaps Joe's responses to her criticism became less defensive. Joe moved from a shaky foundation to a centeredness and peace that improved everything.

Joe did eventually leave this job. He did not expect affirmations to doll up his resume and take him on interviews, though he did think positively when in that process, too. His goal, at first, was simply to be able to endure the Monday-morning meetings. Once he got through that, everything was easier. He knew this job was not right for him forever. When he left the job, however, he was already very successful in his tasks and his employer hated to see him go. Plus, he didn't leave angry, saying, "I'm glad to get out of here," or burn bridges. He went from a platform of centeredness to a new platform of centeredness.

It is suggested that when you use affirmations, you don't gear them to be extremely specific to your situation. That's directing divine order to go your way instead of its own right way. Here's an example of the suggested open-mindedness you use with your affirmations:

REPLACE

I WILL RECEIVE A 10 PERCENT RAISE.

WITH

MY GOOD WILL COME TO ME.

REPLACE

I WILL GET A NEW JOB THIS MONTH.

WITH

I WILL BE DIRECTED ON THE RIGHT PATH AT THE RIGHT TIME.

REPLACE

MY BOSS WILL SEE THE LIGHT AND TREAT ME NICELY.

WITH

I WILL BE CENTERED AND IN THE FLOW IN ALL CIRCUMSTANCES.

Another benefit of this type of affirmation is that it does not limit your choices. You might believe one way, such as getting a new job this month, is the right way. Perhaps you can think of no other better alternative. Yet one might exist beyond your vision. Sometimes, using these "open-minded" affirmations helps you develop even more alternatives to the situation.

Please don't let this advice worry you about doing affirmations the "right" way. Any positive thought is good. There are affirmations you can use in various sections of this book, specifically designed for work-related challenges: dealing with others, handling your duties, achieving prosperity, and more. If you like, take a highlighter and mark the ones you especially like. Think of your own, too. Keep them in a positive-thinking notebook. Copy affirmations from other sources that you think are especially pertinent.

Affirmations will work for you, regardless of the situation you are facing. Speak the words aloud or think them. Eventually you'll memorize several. One quick one that I use for anything is, "I am whole, well and free." That just about says it all!

Start off with these, to get you centered and at peace regarding your work situation:

RIGHT TIMING IS IN EFFECT IN MY LIFE. ALL THINGS ARE OCCURRING AS THEY SHOULD.

MY HEART RELEASES FEELINGS OF

TROUBLE AND FILLS WITH THE PEACE
OF PATIENCE.

WHEREVER I AM, WHATEVER I DO, A
HIGHER POWER IS WITH ME.

DIVINE JUSTICE IS AT WORK
NOW AND FOREVER.

I SEEK THE GOOD, BE IT A TRICKLE OR A
ROARING RIVER, IN EVERY SITUATION.

THE PLAN FOR MY DIRECTION IS WITHIN
ME, READY AT THE RIGHT TIME.

I AM FREE FROM THE PAST—FREE FROM
PAST MISTAKES, ASSUMPTIONS, WRONG
THINKING AND LIMITED CONCEPTS.
ALL IS NEW!

I AM ATTUNED TO THE RHYTHM OF SUCCESS.

MY IDENTITY IS NOT DEFINED BY WORK BUT BY WHO I AM. AND I AM WONDERFUL!

ALL I SEE IS OPPORTUNITY!

How do you cut the external negative input? First, find the influences in your life. Since all my good friends are positive thinkers, I'm lucky. I found that I received much negative input from the "news"—TV, radio, the newspaper. That solution was easy. I watch TV, but not the news. I don't have time to listen to my radio because in my car I'm always playing an affirmation tape or a "book on tape." And I don't subscribe to the newspaper any longer—that helps the environment. Perhaps I'm not up on news as some people are, but I also miss the constant stream of information about murders, car accidents, sex scandals, struggles among government leaders, etc.

Some people have told me their relatives are a negative influence. Perhaps you have gone home for a holiday and reverted to the role of a child, being told you "can't" or being belittled. Some people have readjusted their relationships with parents, siblings or other relatives by explaining what's missing in the relationship. Others don't want to at this point. In that case, they were better off not going home for the holidays. They made other plans (some decide to travel) and actually felt much better!

Identify these influences and take the unusual path, if you need to. Some "obligations" are only such because you make them so. One woman decided to leave an organization she was volunteering for—she felt she "should" volunteer but it was too negative an experience. She took a break from it for a while, then volunteered for something else. Guess what? She was a much better volunteer the second time around anyway. The situation was better.

You don't always have to go head-to-head with negative situations and people. I choose to explain to another my feelings if that person directs negativity to me. Others in a situation might want to just avoid the situation. If so, okay. Take your right path.

Remember to fill your mind with the good after releasing the bad. If you don't want your mind to say, "you can't," give it something else to say! Like, "I can"! This replacement theory works the same way as the canceling technique described earlier. Just as in worrying about battling negative thoughts might give them more power, trying to extract negative thoughts without replacing them might give your mind nothing to do but to turn to what it knows—negativity! So always replace outgoing negative patterns with affirmations and good thinking.

Find additional materials to fill yourself with wonderful thoughts. Uplifting books, as well as audio and videotapes, can be a great boost. You might like subliminal tapes or tapes featuring calming music and nature sounds. You might prefer straight texts about Jesus and his great works, or general life-affirming books. Once you get into the mode of looking for good stuff, you'll even find certain novelists whose works give you a positive feeling; musicians whose songs are affirmations; and scientists who report of marvelous findings that suggest the validation of a benevolent, cooperative universe. These more general forms of education and entertainment can also be life-affirming.

There will be "up" and "down" days as you go through the workhealing process. But congratulate yourself. You are making it. Like the seas, progress sometimes ebbs and flows. You are on the right pathway. You are reaching for even more of your own good.

LET'S AFFIRM:

ANXIETY AND WORRY FALL AWAY AS I
TURN WITHIN AND ACCEPT PEACE.

MY HEART RELEASES FEELINGS OF TROU-
BLE AND FILLS WITH THE PEACE
OF PATIENCE.

INFINITE GOOD IS ABUNDANTLY MINE.
I CLAIM IT NOW.

WHEN YOU FEEL YOU'RE OPERATING ON RAW EMOTION

Circumstances can pull a variety of feelings out of us, taking us on an unpredictable roller coaster ride. Moods swing quickly and mercilessly.

But I can pull myself together and be centered in the knowledge that I can move onto a level platform.

Rather than express all emotions, I go within and collect myself. I see myself moving onto a firm and sure foundation. I become a radiant expression of strength and self-control.

The future holds for me full control of my emotions, regardless of the circumstances that occur. I do not compromise my feelings just because I can withhold an emotional display. I remain all that I am, and move forward on a plane of confidence and inner strength.

WHEN YOU WANT TO STAY POSITIVE

I take this time, right now, to focus my energy and love on positive thinking. Despite the past or current events, I can stay firmly rooted in a positive way of thinking and believing.

When the weather is rainy, I will realize that it's not a "gray day"—the Earth is nourishing itself. When another person seems less than welcoming, I will realize that it is only temporary or unimportant. When challenges arise before me, I will remember that I have worked through and learned from other past experiences. In all situations, I remain positive.

I am filled with the bright light and resonating vibrancy of positive light. May my positive light shine within me and out from me to bless others.

WHEN YOU'RE HAVING TROUBLE STAYING POSITIVE

Even more difficult than thinking positive is to realize the full power of positive thinking and not being able to do it as I would like. However, I now take this opportunity to know that I can do it. I can change the tide of negative thinking and erase its wrong effect from my life. I can replace negative actions and thoughts with powerful affirmative thinking.

As I move forward on this journey, I think of negative thoughts as fleeting birds. If I am sitting in a room conversing with someone and a bird flies by, I might be aware of it but do not give it my attention. Those fleeting birds are like my negative thoughts. During the course of my day, I might be aware of negative thoughts, but they will quickly pass by and I will remain centered in my task. I will retain my new, upgraded way of thinking and living.

WHEN YOU FEAR LOSING YOUR JOB

Circumstances seem to indicate a negative future for my job position. Concerns about firing, layoff or the closure of a department or organization fuel worries about my future days in this position.

I now release those worries and concerns. All images relating to this worry are falling away from me now. Replacing the worries and stress is a calm, glowing light within—a light of knowing hope, filling me and staying in me. This releasing light gives me reassurance, lets me know that all circumstances will have their right outcome.

As I prepare for work and do my job, I retain this calm assurance within—regardless of outer circumstances—knowing that I am secure and strong. My calm assurance surrounds me and protects me.

WHEN YOU HAVE LOST A JOB

What is traditionally a time of despair and despondency—losing a job—will be turned around by me. I turn my thoughts away from losing a job, from blaming myself or others. I give thanks for experience gained and from having grown through this experience. I will now move forward to a higher plateau.

I have not "lost" a job—instead, I have gained a new opportunity of freedom to seek something on a higher and better level for me. God guides me on this search, giving me patience, ability and confidence.

I rise and meet a new day in my life—a new day of new sunshine, new growth and new opportunities.

5

Abundant Time and Energy

*Q*uotas are a part of every day for many people. There are expected numbers of pieces to be made per hour, people to be seen, or cash to be earned. In some cases, it's a necessary system but at times it seems like a necessary evil.

Even where no quotas exist there can be pressure. Pressure, too, has its place. Imagine if the workplace had no specific goals and just progressed willy-nilly in a jelly-fish sort of way until something got done. The company would go out of business, employees would be confused and aimless, and we'd be living in a world of lower-quality products and services.

When there is too much pressure at work, though, we feel it. Time and energy become extremely precious com-modities—even to the executive who has the financial capability of quitting his job!

When you feel boxed in by the pressures of time and energy, remember that there really are no limits to the time and energy of the world. We view time as 24 hours per day, but that's based on the sun's rotation around the earth. Time really began and ends with eternity.

You might be thinking, how does this help me? Well, knowing the true spectrum of time is a great first start. One person who worked in a factory and constantly felt pressured by a quota of producing 600 pieces per hour practically fell apart at the end of the day. He was always worried about time—making the 600 pieces per hour—and felt his energy was in a constant state of near-depletion.

He couldn't just make the number of pieces per hour he chose; his job security depended on making the quota. What he soon realized, though, was that his worry was draining his energy—not the job, or even the quota. As he worked, he watched the clock, or his watch, and worried, worried, worried about whether he'd make the quota that hour. Sometimes there was brief relief five minutes before the hour, when he could see that the counter on his machine had already passed the 600 mark.

He decided to do his best. He did not worry. He watched the clock less and less. His feeling about his energy level improved, and he did make his quotas.

Sometimes withdrawals on our time and energy come from other people, not systems or places. When this occurs, we again must take a step back, see the bigger picture, and start from there. There is more in the next chapter to help you with the other people who seem to rob you of time and energy.

You've heard it said, "There are only 24 hours in a day."

Or, "a person has only so much energy." Both of these statements imply the same thing: *you have your limits.* Physically, we do. The problem is, we tell ourselves that so much that we limit ourselves even more than we have to. What if someone had told the Wright brothers, "Humankind will never find a way to fly"?

Eliminate the concept of having limited time and energy, even if it seems silly to you to do so. Your mind tells you much. Tell yourself you have abundant time and energy. If you can't think of any other words to use, just affirm that over and over:

I HAVE ABUNDANT TIME AND ENERGY.
I HAVE ABUNDANT TIME AND ENERGY.
I HAVE ABUNDANT TIME AND ENERGY.

It works. That's the reason so many people use affirmations, audiotapes on positive thinking, subliminal tapes, etc. If you tell yourself something long enough, you will believe it. Then you can achieve it.

OTHER WAYS

Take some other measures to help yourself, too. Examine your diet. Medical science has practically proven that a high-fat diet replete with refined sugar slows you down (in more ways than one—it's hard on your immune system, too). Get enough sleep. Simply getting enough sleep can solve problems on its own! Be as physically and mentally healthy as you can be.

Take some clutter out of your schedule, too. There is extra time there. Eliminate something, even if you have to eliminate something you like. Give yourself time. With time comes patience, and with patience comes peace.

One man who was practically a workaholic and who had subsequently burned out decided to stay home with his child. At first, it seemed odd. Every moment seemed a waste of time. He was doing *nothing,* he thought. He played at the park, flew kites, watched cartoons, blew bubbles, etc. As time went on, he relaxed. He didn't worry about what was getting "done." He had time for housework, but he truly was not in a rush. He just had much less to do, and his body and mind had to get adjusted to it.

He entered a new era of realization about himself. He felt more centered than ever. But it was a weird transition for him, because the artificial busyness of the workplace that had absorbed him for so long actually created behavior patterns for him. Those patterns were hard to change.

Many of us would like to be in his situation, too, not having to work outside of running the household. How can you feel you have abundant time and energy when you have a full-time job and a family? There are work chores, home chores, driving kids to and fro, and practically no time for eating and sleeping.

Step 1, I'll repeat, is affirm:

I HAVE ABUNDANT TIME AND ENERGY.

Just talk yourself into it.

Also know that you do not need great chunks of time to do great things. If you're 55 and starting to write your first novel, don't worry that you didn't start earlier. If you're 70 and in college, don't fret that you didn't get the degree sooner. And if you're 20 and want to do great things, remember that you don't necessarily have to work hard from this point to retirement to "get there."

Just know that whatever you want to do in life, *there will be time; you will have the energy.*

I've known some physically and mentally healthy people who were just about as active as humans can get. They weren't natural athletes or lucky people who'd never had problems. Some of them had been in therapy or had gone through a long period of diet and exercise to get to where they were. But their energy is abundant—from morning till night. None of them are under 30, either. They have a bounce in their step and a shine in their eyes. They seldom feel exhausted. And they have plenty of time, as well as plenty of achievements.

Our capabilities are limitless. What we now know we can do is like looking at one star in the sky; what we can really do is like looking at all the stars from a vantage point out in space—stars above, below, and all around us. You are greater than you could ever know. You have more energy within you than you realize. And there really aren't just "24 hours in a day" anyway. Think about it. The one-day concept was invented to make calendars. You have one long continuum of time before you. Step into it.

TO HELP YOU BALANCE WORK AND HOME

Sometimes I feel overwhelmed by the dual demands of work and home.

I take this moment now to relax, to let my worries and cares fall away. I take a slow, deep breath and release. My troubles are fleeing from me now, and I realize the glowing light within.

I am given limitless energy, creative ideas and an abundance of patience as I meet the needs of my home and my work. No longer will I need to frantically tackle chores, busily worrying about how I'll do it all. I can do what I must do.

Whenever I feel tugged by demands, I will slow my pace and remember the endless, enduring ability given to me to achieve all I must achieve. I go forward confidently with that divine knowledge.

TO MAKE TIME WORK FOR YOU, NOT AGAINST YOU

It has been said, "If you want something done, ask a busy person to do it."

But there is no nobility in busyness. I examine myself to see if a rush is part of my life because I feel a need to push myself or feel harried by my duties. It might be a situation where work duties imposed by others make me feel extremely busy.

In any case, I take charge of my time right now. Plenty of time is available to me—time to work, rest and enjoy myself. I begin now to eradicate activities that are making me unnecessarily busy. I begin now to eliminate the feeling that I am rushed all the time.

Time does not "work against me." It is something I fully control, and I now draw myself to the fullest awareness that time works for me.

TO ATTRACT ABUNDANT ENERGY

Let my energy level be at its highest and best, as though I'm perky and alert for a bright new morning.

I banish all thoughts that my energy is limited or depletes in the same way water pours down a drain. My energy is not limited, and using my energy does not necessarily "use it up." Abundant, ever-flowing energy is at the core of my being, fully free for my use every day.

Even in situations where I don't feel motivated, I will draw myself up to maximum energy. In situations where I don't feel productive or wanted, I will still draw upon my endless energy to be the best me that I can be.

Abundant energy is mine—today and every day.

WHEN YOU WANT TO LIVE IN A CENTER OF LIMITLESS TIME AND ENERGY

I do not want each day to stretch me, testing my patience and abilities. Instead, I want each day to surge before me as a fountain of time and energy. I have the time I need to do all things. I have full energy, buoying me through the day and evening.

I visualize myself in a pure column of beaming energy, ever powerful and sizzling with life. I also see myself walking peacefully on the continuum of time, in perfect balance with the harmony of the universe.

I am centered in the flow of limitless time and energy.

AFFIRMATIONS

I HAVE ABUNDANT, EVER-INCREASING, EVER-RENEWING TIME AND ENERGY.

INFINITE REALMS OF PATIENCE LIE WITH-IN ME, GIVING ME STRENGTH.

A GLOWING LIGHT IS ENCIRCLING ME NOW. I FEEL REFRESHED AND RENEWED.

I BEGIN EACH DAY WITH ZEST AND A RENEWED SENSE OF PURPOSE.

I RADIATE LIFE, LIVING JOYFULLY AND CREATIVELY.

I AM FILLED WITH JOY; I AM STRENGTH-ENED AND STRONG AT ALL TIMES.

**THE POWER WITHIN ME IS A FOUNTAIN,
ALWAYS FLOWING, ALWAYS BEAUTIFUL,
ALWAYS REFRESHING.**

**I MOVE THROUGH EACH DAY, ENCIRCLED
BY SIZZLING ENERGY AND LOVE.**

ALL THE TIME IN THE WORLD IS MINE.

6

The Good in All Others

*D*id it ever occur to you that a person that you can't help despising might be loved by another? That a person who treats you in a poor manner might treat someone else kindly and sweetly?

This is a realization we might not want to hold on to, for it forces us to think kind thoughts about someone when it's much easier just to snarl and color him or her in one way.

We are multi-faceted people. We have our good days and some of us have our bad days (some of us are working on a strict eternal schedule of "good days only"). Try to think this way about the supervisor or co-worker who's not treating you so appropriately. If it's just too hard to picture that person being nice to somebody, or being lovable, then realize that *the possibility exists*.

I have a memory of carsickness to share with you. Just what you wanted to hear, right? Yuck! But hold on, it's worth it.

When my family took driving trips during my childhood, I spent a good amount of time getting carsick. I remember one occasion when I was about eight or nine years old, and I can't remember where we were going, when I moaned for my father to stop the car so I could get sick. I stood on the shoulder of the road, doing my gastro business, and half embarrassed that a few blocks away stood an elegant, old-style church. Its white steeple gleamed proudly in the sun. The front yard of the church was filled with people dressed in their Sunday best. Perhaps a picnic was going to take place or people were just visiting after church.

Before I got back in the car, my mother noticed someone approaching us. It was a girl about my age with a glass of water. Her mother had suggested that she bring down the water. I was grateful and drank it.

My brother said, "He'll get better now—that's holy water!"

The point is, that same day, someone was probably envious of this girl and her mother. Perhaps that person was thinking, "Look at them, showing off in their new clothes."

But they were my Good Samaritans. Okay, I was not suffering with leprosy by the roadside, but carsickness can get pretty tedious.

It's an example I try to remember every time I feel anger in a work situation. Maybe I'm having a conflict with that person, but someone else finds that person lovable and wonderful. It's only my perspective.

It's difficult, though, to feel love for a "bad boss." There are books and articles on "how to deal with a bad boss." A disagreeable supervisor seems to come with the territory.

There's a reason this occurs, though. One becomes a supervisor usually because he or she has the necessary dominant skills to manage duties or other people in a superior way. So the boss isn't someone who says, "That's all right—just do it your way," or, "Get that done whenever you feel like it." Also, in 99 percent of situations, your boss has a boss to please.

There are also negative situations with co-workers. The competing constraints on time and resources can clash, especially when you consider the different personalities involved. Two otherwise perfectly nice people can practically get into a dogfight if there are enough conflicts on a project.

For most of history, the workplace has put WORK first and PEOPLE second. Only recently have we begun to see a change. The feelings and opinions of workers are finally getting major consideration. Analysts realize their value for productivity purposes.

But the fact remains: we clash with co-workers, too.

If you're trying to mentally examine "what went wrong," why a boss or co-worker is bothering you, and what you might have done to fuel the situation, stop now. There is not much place in workhealing for self-judgment. Taking a look at how you fit into the problems you experience and what changes you can make is Step Two. First comes the workhealing: blessing and fully loving yourself and all others and all situations. Don't use your energy to analyze; use your energy to heal yourself and your situation. That self-analysis and self-realization can come later.

Also, you are not inactive while waiting for the "Step Two," or self-analysis. You are actively improving your immediate world by blessing yourself and others and by learning to love yourself and others. Once you're on a higher plateau, mentally, you'll be better able to look at your past and your involvement in work experiences and, with kinder self-judgment, objectively see your part in all situations.

When work makes you feel terrible, it's a bad time to assess whether you caused some of your own problems. You're already feeling bad enough! So don't perpetuate the spiral of negative work thoughts with self-analysis right now. Just workheal.

How do you handle day-to-day situations while you're workhealing? Change your ways to use a few simple techniques. First, pay attention to your thoughts when an aggravating incident occurs at work. Read your thoughts. Are they going like this:

He's so stupid!

She's just doing that to bug me!

WHY is an idiot like him in that position?

Can't she calm down?

These thoughts flit by extremely quickly, so you'll have to pay careful attention. Once you've begun this recognition process, change to a technique of releasing those feelings. It's sort of like these thoughts are running toward you and you quickly put up a brick wall to stop them.

THEY'RE IN GOD'S LIGHT

Be patient. It will take time. You will get tired of thinking about it. But the results are marvelous. The first part takes care, like lighting fireworks. The second part is like *watching* fireworks—the glorious result. You stop your thoughts; you relax; you don't spend your mental time battering your boss or co-workers.

Then do your best at seeing them in the light of a Higher Power. This doesn't mean you have to love them; trying to force that on yourself at a time like this might only cause deeper resentment. Just see them bathed in a bright light emanating from above. See this as God's light, for we are all in it.

When they're acting angry toward you, respond calmly—for they're in God's light.

When they're asking you about something, respond honestly—they're in God's light.

When they're making demands on you, collaborate with them in peace—they're in God's light.

This doesn't mean give in. It doesn't mean not to be honest with yourself. It doesn't mean they're always right. It simply means to center yourself in your own perfect God-given strength and see the situation with peace, not judgment. It will be the opposite of what you might tend to do. All of us get defensive when approached forcefully. But anger begets anger, and peace begets peace. Your non-emotional, honest, peaceful responses will very likely dampen the flames of anger that are dancing around the room.

Does this make you a wimp? No. You haven't "given in" or gone against your own beliefs. It doesn't mean that your boss or co-worker is right. It only means that you choose to take the highest and best path for yourself.

BE A CENTER OF GOODNESS

There is one power-packed affirmation that can both give you direction and strengthen you at the same time:

I am a center of goodness, radiating out to all I meet.

Be such a center of goodness. Reach for the goodness within and radiate it out to others. Let go of "goodness," meaning a sugary-sweet, unrealistic personality. Goodness makes up the real you, and there's nothing wrong with it. You'll also have a richer and more sparkling outpouring of love when you think this toward others you haven't had agreeable relations with.

When another raises his or her voice to you, think, **I am a center of goodness, radiating out to all I meet.**

When another accuses you of something you didn't do, think, **I am a center of goodness, radiating out to all I meet.**

If you feel anger from others invading your workplace and your mind, think, **I am a center of goodness, radiating out to all I meet.**

I don't have to do a lot of explaining about what that means. In fact, it has shades of slightly different meanings for different people. Each person sees his or her lacks dwindling away in a different manner while trying to be a center of goodness.

If all of us could have a pure and perfect perception of one another, without any judgment, we'd be living in a world of complete peace—even with the different personalities and interests that we all have. We would all be centers of goodness, radiating out to all we meet (we're already all centers of goodness—but not all of us are radiating it!).

So practice the steps outlined above to handle your difficult supervisor or co-workers:

1. Trace judgmental thoughts.

2. Stop those thoughts as they arrive.

3. See your fellow in a column of pure, bright light, and know that it is the light of the Creator.

4. Respond to the light, letting subjective judgment flow away from you.

5. Be proud of yourself for taking the highest and best pathway in life. Know that you are a center of goodness.

You might never become good friends with your supervisor or co-workers, but you'll be amazed at the difference.

WHEN CONFLICT AT WORK IS DISTRESSING YOU

Conflicts and disagreements at work may have seemed to sap my energy, erode my security, or create negative feelings.

I push aside all thoughts of the past, with negative events and worries crumbling into nothingness. My security is fully restored and glowing with a golden fullness.

Whether conflict continues at work is not a barrier to my happiness or success. I will take the right pathway in my own work, not involving myself in negative situations.

Conflicts will eventually dissolve, with a new, clear understanding shining forth. I stand in confidence and relaxation, knowing that the right outcome in every situation is already beginning.

WHEN YOU FEEL LIKE SOMEONE IS SABO-TAGING YOU

Whether it is reality or my mind operating negatively, I feel that someone is sabotaging me. I choose, at this very moment, to wash away the thoughts of sabotage—the fear, worry and pain.

My thoughts and actions move onto the higher path—the way that is right and good. My mind is clear of all thoughts of being a victim or of getting even. Instead, I let divine justice do its work of adjusting and balancing—knowing that all things eventually have their right outcome.

Whether I confront the person or not is not of concern to me now, for the right outcome will occur. I remain secure in the glow of divine justice. No one can sabotage me, since I work and live in the supreme light of God's love and protection.

TO HANDLE AN UNPLEASANT SUPERVISOR

A supervisor can be a friend and teacher, mentor or inspiration. It's especially hurtful when the boss is unpleasant—whether that unpleasantness is caused by my work or simply by the boss's own situation.

Whatever the case, I release any negative feelings toward myself. I heal myself from hurtful words or actions, knowing that true and real approval comes from myself. I am my true boss, and I am filled with all the knowledge and energy I will ever need.

I see my supervisor surrounded by loving light, also being healed and shown full potential.

I can go forward in a new way, knowing that my worth is at its highest—even if another person approaches me in a negative fashion. I am complete and whole.

WHEN CO-WORKERS SEEM TO WORK AGAINST YOU

Whether my perception is right or wrong, I feel that others are working against me. First, I do not worry whether they really are or whether it just seems so.

Nothing can truly work against me in God's world, because I am a child of God. I now inherit the goodness of His kingdom—goodness that is already mine and will always be with me.

As I comfort myself, knowing that others cannot work against me, I know that divine justice is always served. Though I may not see it, that perfect justice is at work now and always. I need not even do anything to move it along—divine justice works as it should.

I move forward confidently and freely. No one can do me harm.

WHEN YOU FEEL JEALOUS OF ANOTHER

I have felt envy for another. I now recognize that I have my own many, many good qualities. I have made achievements of my own.

Sometimes another might seem to have more than I or have an easier way in life. But at times, I'm unaware that others are thinking that way about me.

We all have our emotional and material ups and downs. We do not need to feel jealous of another, for our good is coming to us. And in our ever-expanding, ever-beautiful world filled with wonder, we can always have good. We don't have to ride the ups and downs of appearances in our world.

I choose now to see, to be and to have all the best that life has to offer. The best is mine.

FOR HANDLING THE HURT CAUSED BY ANOTHER

Another person has hurt me. I stop analyzing why, and now release the hurt. My heart is free; my heart is clear as sparkling crystal.

I forgive. I do not ponder why I was hurt. I just bless the other person. I pray that the person learns to walk on the highest and best path of life. I bless, and I forgive.

My new, free feeling gives me wings, and I fly away from my hurt feelings. I am free, the other person is free, and all is clear now. All is clear.

AFFIRMATIONS

I SEE ALL OTHERS IN THE PURE
CHRIST LIGHT.

WHEN OTHERS CHALLENGE ME, I TURN
WITHIN TO A WARM AND SAFE HAVEN.
ALL IS TURNING TO GOOD AND TO GOD.

I AM A CHANNEL FOR EVER-INCREASING
GOOD IN THE WORLD.

WE ARE ALL ONE WITH A HIGHER
POWER—IN SPIRIT, SOUL AND BODY.
I LOVE OTHERS AS I ACKNOWLEDGE
OUR ONENESS.

I THANK GOD FOR THE GOOD THAT IS
ACCOMPLISHED THROUGH MY WORK
AND THE WORK OF OTHERS.

I FORGIVE OTHERS, AND THIS FORGIVE-
NESS MAKES ME FREE AND WHOLE.

WITHOUT LOSING ANY PART OF WHO I
AM, I ACCEPT AND BLESS ALL OTHERS
IN MY WORLD.

I PRAY FOR OTHERS, SEEING THEM AS
LOVING CHILDREN UNITED WITH
THE POWER OF THE UNIVERSE.

MAY ALL THE GOODNESS OF GOD FLOW
FORTH TO PROSPER ME AND OTHERS.

I SEE THE WORLD AS AN EVER-INCREAS-
ING, EVER-ABUNDANT CIRCLE OF HARMONY
AND JOY.

7

Limitless Prosperity

I have a story to tell you that is not your typical anecdote.

I have always liked to believe that when I think prosperity, prosperity will occur; and when I am feeling desperate, greedy, or negative about prosperity, it will not come my way.

However, it seems that God sometimes likes to throw me a bone.

At least a couple of times in my life I have wanted to give up trying to develop a prosperity consciousness and simply believe that the flow of happiness, material goods and spiritual wealth (all of which make up prosperity) was as wild as the wind. Once I recall being not in desperate

▼

financial straits, but feeling as if year to year my financial picture was static. I didn't even have the six months of cash in a savings account for emergency "if you lose your job" that some financial experts suggest. (Of course, as soon as I decided I didn't like that concept, I had the money—but that's another story.)

I was in a multi-day funk, knowing that in a few days I'd probably pull myself out of the doom and gloom but also feeling strong inertia. I said a silent, quick prayer, something like, "God, just surprise me with some big good thing—not some lesson or realization." It sounds terrible, but I really wanted something materially significant and a total surprise.

Two days later, I got a certified letter from the bank. Return receipt requested. Thinking I had really misbalanced my checkbook this time and possibly bounced checks from here to Schenectady, my heart pounded as I opened the letter.

I won $2,500!

The most I had ever won in any sort of contest before was a Butterball Turkey.

The bank had been giving away money to promote its services, and I had entered the contest without thought. I am not normally the type who enters contests, gambles, or buys lottery tickets because I like to live and move in the world of practicality and self-achievement.

I'm not suggesting that you begin praying for major chunks of money to come falling from the sky, because you might be disappointed. But there might be some truth to the matter that a Higher Power not only helps you gain prosperity when you help yourself and are positive, but also when you need it and aren't quite "up to par" in your positive-thinking efforts.

SIMPLE CONFIDENCE

How does it work that when we believe we are prosperous, suddenly lack is out of our life and we truly get prosperous? It's simple confidence. We settle more happily within ourselves, looking at the abundance we already have, and feel better. Then we gain more.

It might seem some people in this world cannot see the abundance they already have. What if you're homeless? Starving? Is thinking about prosperity a mockery then? No. For everyone has some sort of prosperity within. If you have a sound mind and reasonably like yourself, you are well ahead of much of the world—even if you're financially broke!

See all there is that shows you have abundance. Take a moment now to write ten great things you now have in your life. Remember, prosperity and abundance are not just money, but all good things. You can list friends, family, pets, even hobbies you like, or whatever.

The one thing that might be missing from your list is happiness with work or a feeling that work makes you prosperous. But even if your work doesn't pay what you think it should, you are receiving much from it—no matter how much you "hate" your job!

Many times we feel our pay isn't adequate because we don't like the job. If you've ever had a job you truly loved, you can remember how secondary the pay became. You might have said, "I wish I got paid more—but I love it anyway." Enjoying other people at work, and the tasks, can supersede the financial gain any day.

But that doesn't mean the two are mutually exclusive. You can have it all—a great job with satisfying co-workers and a wonderful boss, PLUS terrific duties AND great pay. We've all been taught that we must "work hard" to "get ahead." Or that "good things don't come easily."

Not true. Our society is structured so that gains in pay come with increased knowledge, skills and experience, but that doesn't mean it happens that way 100 percent of the time. Also, good things DO come easily—to those who believe. Expect good and you will get it.

LEAVE THE LACK BEHIND
One of the greatest crises we can have is our view of money. Now remember, money isn't everything, but we do need it to function in our society. And often, a little more can make functioning in our society a little easier.

What's the view most people have of money? It's:

—Money doesn't grow on trees (I won't refute that!)

—Money is scarce.

—A chosen few are lucky enough to have abundant money.

—You work hard all your life, then you're secure.

—Money comes and money goes.

The value of a prosperity consciousness is that regardless of what's in your checking account, your mental account can always be filled to the brim! Prosperity is yours in abundance. The only cost is simply realizing it's there—and that's an easy charge to pay.

Be filled with a prosperity consciousness, and you'll attract money to yourself. It can come about in various ways. Perhaps your job will pay more or you'll get a new job that pays more. Maybe you'll win something. Perhaps you'll find a new way to earn extra money. It might come in some unanticipated way that has nothing to do with your work or with winning!

Don't view money as scarce. Don't feel guilty if you receive it. If money was wrong, would it have been given to us? The only fault with money is *when people misuse it.* When greed is expressed, when money is used to gain negative personal power, when money consumes a person—these are times when money is wrong. Having it is not.

So feel good about the better financial picture you can create for yourself. And right now, begin with a strong prosperity consciousness.

You have much; you will continue to receive much. You are prosperous!

WHEN MONEY SEEMS "TIGHT"

I will eradicate the feeling that money is "tight" or scarce or more easily flows to other people. I rest in the knowledge that money is not tight in any circumstance. Prosperity does not more easily flow to other people; it is available, in full, to all people.

Perhaps in the past I've had times of lack or have had challenges in building my own prosperity. Perhaps I've had difficulty in building my own prosperity consciousness. But let me now know the truth: that all-encompassing prosperity is available to all people.

When thoughts arise that make me believe that my prosperity is limited, or that I'm having some sort of shortage at this time, let me realize, God, the fullness of my life.and the truth that all good things can come to me. Let me completely eliminate the belief that money is "tight" or that prosperity cannot be mine. Let my mind be free and clear to accept the truth that money is not tight and that prosperity is mine, beginning now.

TO ERASE CONCERN ABOUT MONEY

Quite often, we equate our money with work. We ponder what others make, how much more we can make, and how we compare—as well as our past and future amounts of income. Yet true riches are not cash at all, and being centered will bring everything I need—without any call to worry about it.

I rest in a sense of peaceful centeredness, knowing that what I need, as well as what I have truly earned, will come to me—despite any current appearances of lack. I attract to myself the prosperity that helps make work rewarding.

My focus is now shifted away from goods that I want to a sense of well-being about my income. For a sense of well-being is the foundation for goods that I want anyway. My rewards will come to me, even as I focus on a sense of prosperity that is already within.

My true riches are a strength and knowing within. These true riches do not waver or wane, even if there are days I don't feel up to par. My true riches stay within, regardless of what happens with surface issues—my salary, or what others earn. Even if I do not have a job, my true riches are there; they are mine. They are what I need and all I need because they come from God.

I am prosperous!

TO BREAK FROM A PAST LACK

In the past, I have felt a void in my life, a void in the area of prosperity. But it was not truly something that I was lacking materially, it was only a lack created by my own lack of prosperity consciousness. I now understand that despite appearances of what has happened in the past, I can create my own world through divine mind. And I reconnect my consciousness with divine mind and affirm the truth of that link.

I will never again have a feeling of lack in my life. I will never again have a time period of lack in my life.

For those challenges are behind me now. I know fully that with divine mind, I will have a perfect prosperity consciousness—beginning this moment! From this moment on, I have eliminated the lack in my life. I live with a rich and full feeling of prosperity that stands me in good stead, now and every day in the future. I am thankful for this renewed, complete and seamless prosperity consciousness.

FOR ELIMINATING YOUR GUILT IN WANTING PROSPERITY

I feel guilty that I am asking for prosperity and wanting prosperity. But let me now realize that there is no need for this guilt. For I am not asking for anything that will hurt our world. Nor am I asking for anything that I am not meant to have. I simply want the highest and best in life.

I am not greedy because I ask for prosperity or for material goods. I do not ask that others have any sort of lack, I only ask that good things happen for all people.

I now push out thoughts of guilt. Guilt is unproductive and unnecessary, helping no one—not myself nor others. I empty my mind of all feelings of guilt. I let enter into my mind the pure, unfiltered feeling that I want complete prosperity for myself, others and my world.

Now I rest my mind, knowing that I no longer need guilt or negative feelings regarding this matter. Those feelings are gone. My mind is filled with the clear and perfect knowledge that I can freely ask for and receive prosperity. I ask for it, I feel good about asking for it, and it will become mine.

WHEN YOU WANT ABUNDANCE, BUT DON'T WANT TO FEEL GREEDY

My mind guides me in understanding that true abundance is all around me and part of this world. I can have abundance unlimited, because "abundance" doesn't mean I want a mountain of money or material goods to best others. Abundance is a state that can be possessed by all people.

I no longer feel that I am greedy. I just want to reach my fullest potential and have optimum abundance. Optimum abundance is not mutually exclusive. Each of us can have complete abundance because we live in a perfect universe.

WHEN YOU FEEL YOU'LL NEVER BE PROSPEROUS

Past experiences and a seeming future lack have made me feel that I'll never be prosperous. I release those negative thoughts.

Even without material change, I now claim prosperity—in that split second. It is now mine. I now accept prosperity and attract it to myself. I am not lacking. And I know that this new, lustrous countenance will boost me to newer and higher ways of thinking.

77

My inner knowledge is solid: I am prosperous now and forever.

AFFIRMATIONS

**PROSPERITY IS ABUNDANTLY MINE—
I CLAIM IT NOW.**

**MY GOOD FLOWS TO ME NATURALLY AND
EASILY. I ACCEPT MY GOOD
AS IT ARRIVES.**

**THE ACTIONS I TAKE ARE A HIGHER
BEING WORKING THROUGH ME TO BRING
ABUNDANCE TO ME.**

**ATTUNED TO THE ABUNDANCE OF THE
UNIVERSE, I AM PROSPERED.**

**I AM INSPIRED WITH DIVINE IDEAS THAT
BLESS AND PROSPER ME.**

**I HAVE A LIMITLESS SOURCE OF GOOD;
I AM PROSPEROUS.**

THERE IS NO LACK IN DIVINE ORDER; I LIVE IN DIVINE ORDER AND I RECEIVE ALL I NEED.

I AM LED TO NEW IDEAS THAT WILL ENRICH MY LIFE.

MY PURE GOODNESS FLOWS FORTH TO PROSPER ME AND OTHERS.

I AM ONE WITH THE RADIANT LOVE OF THE UNIVERSE, WHICH FILLS MY EVERY NEED.

I AM INSPIRED TO LIVE A SUCCESSFUL LIFE BY THE PROSPERING POWER WITHIN.

8

Fulfilling Duties

*E*verywhere, workplaces are changing. Why? Because people want to kindle their passion. We are departing from the days when one feels he or she is the "breadwinner" and must stay in an unsatisfying job to support others. Kindling your passion does require risk, after all. More people are dismissing the attitude of, "This is the best I can get." People are *thinking*—exploring ways to make a living doing what they want. People are *risking*—jumping toward the possibilities that will enrich their lives. People are *doing*—they are landing securely on their feet in a job that they love and which pays appropriately.

It all comes down to work's *duties*. Our tasks, responsibilities and challenges shape our job. Perhaps our duties are even more important than our pay or co-workers. Haven't you been in a situation where you loved what you were doing but weren't happy with others or the income? When you love what you do, you can tolerate—and outwait—other negative situations.

Why do we stay stuck in a job that has duties we don't enjoy? Our inertia is usually caused by self-talk that keeps us in our places:

"This is the best I can get."

"I won't get better pay somewhere else."

"I'm too old to start over."

"At least I'm comfortable here."

"I should be grateful I have a job."

"This is easier than starting a new job and trying to fit in at a new place."

"Maybe my boss [or a certain co-worker] will quit."

"It's too late to start a new career."

This self-talk shouldn't "keep you in your place" because *this isn't your place.*

Your rightful place is employment that affords you wonderful duties—a place where your passion is kindled!

Start now to change inertia self-talk to positive self-talk that will uplift you and direct you anew:

I can find my rightful place.

I can have it all.

I will find a job that's perfect.

I have the flexibility to try new things.

I have the capability of learning new things.

My path will be smoother and easier than I've ever dreamed.

It's never too late.

I can do better and better in life.

I am entitled to my good—and I will receive it.

This type of redirection will give you a countenance of success. And it goes beyond just appearance and feeling. You truly will transform your path.

Sometimes, we leave one job and later, in the new job, find that things are the same. One reason is that we didn't take the crucial step to center and evaluate what we want before moving on to the new job.

DREAM!

Take time to relax in a quiet spot and think about what you really want to do. Do not allow anxiety to enter your thoughts. Do not think about any limitations—geography, money or the like. *Dream about what you want to do.* You might need several of these sessions to develop your ideas. Truly picture what you want, visualizing your success in that area.

From that point, you can logically assess what you need to do; what you need to learn; the timeframe involved. You can actually begin the process of transforming your life toward a job you love. And don't worry—the money and delightful boss and co-workers can come in the same package.

William knew what it took to jump-start his career. Unfortunately for him, he was stuck jump-starting cars. He had graduated from a two-year college and wanted to get his bachelor's degree in journalism. Why was he "stuck"? The summer after his junior college, he traveled to the university to look around. He didn't see how he could ever afford college, and, since he was close to his family, leave his parents and siblings.

"Most kids are aching to move along at that stage," William said. "But it was scary looking for an apartment that I'd have on my own, or imagine living in the dorm. I knew nobody, and I'd be moving to a large city."

He returned to his hometown and got the only job he could find—working at a store that sold auto parts, hardware, and serviced cars. It was completely out of his element.

Finally, there was one bad day. A customer had laughed out loud when asking for a basic piece of hardware and William had handed him the entirely wrong thing—not knowing the difference. Then William had to mount new tires on a car, a job he wasn't very good at. He virtually endangered himself using the equipment. During his break, William ate a snack on the back steps of the store and watched the setting sun slowly inch its way downward.

"This was it, I realized," William said. "I was 19, worked in a job I hated and didn't know much about, and there wasn't much in life that was exciting."

William managed to spend a few more weeks in the job, but began eyeing the university again. He finally found a dorm room, braced himself, and plunged in. You probably know the end of the story. He graduated from the university, moved on to an even larger city, and was successful. There were some hard times, but he knew he had to survive them to get to a place in life where he could work with duties he liked and make an adequate living.

Stories like this are hard to hear if you feel stuck in your job, burdened with duties you don't like, and have been trying hard to move on. There are many books and other materials about finding a new job or assessing what you want to do, etc. Just don't forget the first step: *workhealing your way out of hating your duties*. It might take time, and you don't want to rush out of your current job just for the sake of rushing.

Learn to love your duties.

What? Yes, no matter what your duties are, bless them for being the work you need to do, and know that your rightful path is before you. Don't be anxious about taking the first step. In deciding to live with your duties for the present moment, you have already taken the first step. Opportunities will open up, and your steps will become lighter and freer.

Imagine you could see the certain future and know one of two things was going to happen:

1. You would leave your current job immediately and find a job that is 50 percent better. You would be in your second job for five years.

2. You would stay in your current job another six months (though that seems agonizing) but then would move to a perfect job!

Wouldn't you pick #2? Have tolerance, patience, and do your job lovingly. Bless your work, even if it doesn't seem to be blessing you. Make peace with your work, with your duties. Not only will it center you more strongly, it will help you make it positively through the time you are in your current job. It will also keep you clear-headed and rational as you seek other employment or assess what direction you need to take.

Believe it or not, all work duties have their function in your life. All tasks build some sort of value in you. Even housework gives you something you didn't have before and gives you something you'll need in the future. Don't toil to try to figure out what. Trust divine order to take care of that.

When you are at work and face a new, hard task, or the "same old drudge-work" tasks, take heart, for everything you're doing is useful. Even if you are doing the same duties over and over each day, you are learning something new each day (even if you don't know what it is!) and are building value for the future. You will use everything. You will.

WHEN YOU FEEL OVERWORKED

The ever-circling demands and tensions of work swirl away from me as I slow myself, breathe deeply, and grant myself a respite from work.

I send peace to those who contribute to my workload, helping them to gain a higher understanding of the amount of work that truly needs to be done.

I do not panic at thoughts of work to be done. I am given energy and organization as I work. I give myself a new peace that I carry with me at all times— a peace to ward off stress and hurry when work seems to be on "overload."

My yoke will be easy and my burden light.

WHEN YOU'VE MADE A BIG MISTAKE

The residue of making a mistake—embarrassment, shame, guilt, self-doubt—will not advance me to a higher place in life. I rid myself of this unwanted residue, knowing I must press forward and move on in life.

The word mistake *is unnaturally serious and given too much power, and I now realize that. It is merely a mis-take, a misstep, a learning experience caused only by trying to create a right outcome. I allow myself to have this mis-take, for I have grown through it. And I realize I cannot create a right outcome. It is already created, and only has to come to me.*

A clear, bright light is shining in and through me

now, illuminating me with new light and new life. My
pathway is before me, and I know I will progress
down that pathway, picking myself up when there is
any sort of impediment. I will learn, grow and enrich
my life along the way. I will even be strengthened, progressing smoothly to my higher good.

FOR A LACK OF MOTIVATION

At times, my work seems lackluster, unfulfilling,
unexciting. Whether or not I should switch jobs or do
something more interesting is not my focus right now.

Instead, I go within, to the realization that all legitimate work helps fulfill the creation process. I can
rise from a lack of interest and boredom to be motivated to go to work and do a good job.

I have been lovingly provided with work—work
that needs my mind and physical ability to be complete. I give fully of myself, knowing that I move forward, and I naturally create more motivation on an
ongoing basis.

I move forward with my work, expressing enthusi-
asm and zeal as I complete day-to-day tasks.

WHEN YOU'RE DOING WRONG AT WORK

Beginning right now, I choose to clean and freshen
my life. I ask for forgiveness and am granted forgiveness for the actions I have taken in the past.

Clouds of guilt, shame and regret fall away from

me as I receive a bright infilling of Spirit. The past is gone—today I am a new person, of new body and mind, taking on a new direction in my work.

Let past wrong actions leave me now and forever. I turn my attention to the power within and let this power within guide me as I make choices at work. All is well and all is for good as I make right choices.

AFFIRMATIONS

I ACHIEVE AND BELIEVE.

I ACT WITH PEACE, LOVE, UNDERSTAND-ING, AND DIVINELY GUIDED ACTION.

NONRESISTANCE IS AN OPEN GATEWAY TO GOOD; I TAKE THAT GATEWAY NOW.

I AM AN ACTIVE PARTICIPANT IN THE UNI-VERSE'S PLAN OF UNFOLDING GOOD.

I BLESS MY WORK, AND MY WORK BLESSES ME.

I AM GIVEN A POSITIVE ATTITUDE AND CHEERFUL MANNER; I CARRY THIS ATTI-TUDE WITH ME AT ALL TIMES.

INNER PRODUCTIVITY RUNS RAMPANT IN MY LIFE; I ACHIEVE FOR MYSELF AND BELIEVE IN MYSELF.

I BLESS MY WONDERFUL ABILITIES.

I USE THE CREATIVE, IMAGINATIVE AND LOVING POWER THAT I HAVE BEEN GIVEN.

I OPEN MY MIND TO A NEW, ENRICHED LIFE.

9

Peace-Filled Progress

*B*race yourself. Just when you've accepted your duties, blessed your supervisor and co-workers, feel that you have abundant time and energy, you might get an "Is that all there is?" feeling. You've workhealed and you feel much better—"now where's my new situation!?!"

This can be the hardest part of the process, if you let it.

It will come. The position you desire, the position that is rightfully yours, will come to you. Maybe you have done all the steps discussed so far. Maybe you've done them in a stellar way. If you still haven't obtained the ideal job position, or have moved into another job position that isn't satisfactory, hold fast, because your good is swooping toward you faster than you can imagine.

Too many times, someone changes and lives in a positive, fulfilling way, then doesn't get the desired result and slips back into old ways. Old ways might seem easier because we've always been that way and it takes time to learn and execute new ways of life. But it's not truly easier to slide back. You can be a whole new you, with whole new results. So stay steadfast.

If you are in this waiting period, bolster the good results you've had so far. Continue to see your duties, time, energy, boss and co-workers in the light of God. Show yourself that you can practice what you preach. You only have yourself, and the world, to help by doing so.

Pray for patience if waiting for your good seems to be like riding on a rough road. Your good is coming. You deserve it. You will receive it.

WHEN YOU SEEM UNABLE TO GO TO ANOTHER JOB

I have had desires to go to another work position but feel lack and even disappointment.

Those feelings of lack are leaving me now; disappointment is leaving me now. I am filled with a fresh new spirit of ease and mobility.

I let go and let divine order show me the right path. I do not toss and turn thoughts of where, when and how in my mind. My desires to move to another job will have the right outcome.

My fresh new spirit of ease and mobility gives me patience and new inner direction. I am being steered onto the right path, and I rest in that knowledge.

WHEN CIRCUMSTANCES SEEM TO HALT YOUR AMBITION

Divine order is what I affirm for myself now and in the future. Though past experiences might have seemed to pull me back, those times and such feelings are no longer part of me.

I trust a Higher Power to lead and guide me in whatever future direction I should take. I will not project ideas of "when" or "how" my ambition will be fulfilled. Rather, I will think "divine order" at times of impatience and let nature take its course.

Knowing that I am steered in the direction I need to go, I rest in divine order.

WHEN YOU NEED A SENSE OF FUTURE DIRECTION

Sometimes, when we think about our future direction, the picture that we see is as foggy and thick as murk by a lake. It is unclear, we are uncertain where we are going, we may feel frightened or confused. But all of this is not needed.

I am not in a position where I cannot *know my future direction. It is often said that "you can't know what the future holds." However, this actually is an untruth in our divine world. Though I may not know the specific instances, people, or changes that will come about in the future, I can know that my direction will be a positive one, that I will continue to move upward and upward to newer heights—newer vistas of living fully.*

Regardless of the details that will occur, and those details are minor, I can know that what is planned for me is a beautiful, tremendous, exciting future filled with opportunities. The direction I need and seek is my own inner direction on what to know, what types of decisions to make. And I can pray for that type of help.

I now ask for the wisdom and understanding to make right choices that affect my future, to help me plan my goals for the future, and give me the knowledge to achieve my goals.

I now know that what is "in the stars" for me is the right outcome, the right outcome for what I choose and wish. I accept the knowledge that the right result is in the works for me. I no longer worry about my future direction, because I know that my future direction is on the highest and best path.

WHEN YOU ARE WORRIED ABOUT THE FUTURE

I have worried about the future—about prosperity, finding the right and fulfilling duties for me, striking the right balance between work and home, perhaps about the effects that such activity will have on me and my dear ones. But now I set those thoughts aside, much as I set aside an empty box that I no longer need.

I now break the habit of worrying about the future. It is only that—a bad habit—and not reality about the future. Whenever I feel worry about the future, I will simply affirm the words divine order. *If worries arrive about prosperity, I will think,* divine order. *If thoughts arise about finding the right duties, I say,* divine order. *If any other types of worries appear, I affirm,* divine order. *I dismiss the negative thoughts from my mind and let my mind fill with clearness and beauty.*

I do not worry about the future. My future holds bright opportunities for me. I embrace the future. It is a wonderful thing that is happening to me now and forever.

AFFIRMATIONS

THE RIGHT OUTCOME IS UNFOLDING IN MY WORLD.

MY PATH WILL BE ILLUMINATED. I STAND READY TO GO DOWN MY PATH OF GOOD.

I PUT MYSELF IN THE LISTENING STILL-NESS, OPEN TO SELF-ELEVATING DIRECTION.

GREATER GOOD IS AWAITING ME NOW.

MY UNLIMITED PATIENCE IS GOD-GIVEN AND GOD-SUSTAINED.

I AM DIVINELY DIRECTED; I ACCEPT DIVINE DIRECTION.

A PATTERN OF GOOD IS UNFOLDING IN
MY LIFE; I REST IN THE KNOWLEDGE
THAT MY GOOD WILL COME TO ME.

NOTHING IS IMPOSSIBLE FOR ME.

I KEEP ON KEEPING ON, THROUGH THE
UNWAVERING STRENGTH THAT IS MINE
NOW AND FOREVER.

I TRUST IN RIGHT OUTCOMES.

I WALK IN THE NEWNESS OF LIFE.

10

Now You Are Healed: Be Free!

*M*y friend, even if you feel just about the same way you did when you started reading this book, you have traveled light-years. It is likely, however, that you've experienced some mental breakthroughs, maybe even more physical freedom, as a result of going through the workhealing process.

Workhealing does not have to be a constant in your life. However, it's always there if you need it. If you are still not in your optimum work situation, keep workhealing. Keep the process going until you reach the place that you need to reach.

If you need to use workhealing again in another job position, that's all right. It is a new and powerful tool for you to possess and have at your command at any time. Using it does not mean you have slid back or failed. Remember: life, like the seas, ebbs and flows. Just know that you have a new and wonderful means of elevating your life to its highest potential.

Until you reach that perfect job experience, keep praying. Pray for those who work for you and those who seem to work "against" you, and for yourself. Stay centered in the light that is within, your true self. Know that your mind is connected with divine mind. No matter what seemingly negative event happens, you can stay centered in a pure and strong column of light, a light that is all around you and within you.

Workhealing is an interesting circle, because at the same time, you are healed and healing. By now your work circumstance may not have changed, and you only feel a small bit better. But you are workhealed—and you can continue to workheal. Press on, till you reach your goal.

Life is not a race. Workhealing is not measured by instant success or long-term continuity. Some situations will require less time and effort and others will need more. The quality of you is not measured by how hard you must work at it. Let all judgment go. Be a source of unlimited help and healing for yourself.

Workhealing is always there for you, whenever you need it. Like an oasis, beckoning with cool and sweet water, workhealing is there to refresh you whenever you want to call on it.

May the best that life has to offer you come to you. Bless you. I love you.

ABOUT THE AUTHOR

CHARLES MALLORY is a full-time writer and editorial consultant who often addresses work-related issues. He was formerly an editor at Unity School of Christianity, where he worked on DAILY WORD, UNITY Magazine, and Unity Books.

He is the author of two previous books, PUBLICITY POWER (Crisp Books, 1989) and DIRECT MAIL MAGIC (Crisp Books, 1991), and he has published more than 100 articles. He is a graduate of the Univerity of Missouri-Columbia.

Mr. Mallory lives in Kansas City with his wife, Joyce Lofstrom, and their two sons, John-Mark and Max.